Fun with Ground Poles
Starring
Tristan the Wonder Horse

1

Foreword

All I was doing was trying to find something to entertain Tristan during another long, cold, Wisconsin winter. Who would have thought what started out as a fun video, intended to amuse my students and Facebook friends, would turn into a viral sensation. What can I say; Tristan became a super star overnight. Creating this book and coming up with new ideas has been nothing but fun, and I have been overwhelmed with the outpouring of support from all over the world. I hope that this is just the beginning. This book is intended to introduce you to the basics of ground pole work, and contains the building blocks to Tristan's elaborate patterns. I hope that everyone enjoys riding these exercises as much as I have enjoyed creating them. Your horse can be a superstar too!

- Kelley Shetter-Ruiz (Tristan's Mom)

Safety First!

We have created this book with horse and rider safety in mind. Please ensure you and your horse are in good health, and physically able to do ground pole exercises before attempting the exercises in this book. We ask that you please wear a helmet while riding, and keep your horse's safety in mind by using boots or bandages to protect your horse's legs. Horses are innately dangerous, and anything can happen. If you or your horse have never done ground pole work before, we suggest consulting with a trainer before attempting these exercises by yourself. We hope these exercises challenge you, and allow you to do something exciting and new with your horse, while bettering both horse and rider.

Table of Contents

Dedicated to my Wonder Horse, Tristan Carpe Diem - you are that horse...

"Great horses are not often easy horses. They have big egos, and idiosyncrasies, and quirks, and foibles. Horses of a lifetime do exist, but only for riders so skillful, tactful, and courageous that they can unlock and then reveal the brilliance of their equine partners."
-Denny Emerson, USEA Hall of Fame Rider

Introduction to Ground Pole Work

Benefits of Ground Pole Work

Ground pole work is often seen as something only done to prepare horses for jumping, but is an activity that can benefit horses and riders of any discipline! Ground pole work has many benefits, such as:

- Assisting horses in strengthening their hind end.
- Helping to develop your horse's rhythm and tempo.
- Improving surefootedness.
- Teaching your horse to focus.
- Improving horse and rider balance.
- It is fun for horse and rider!

Those are just a few of the reasons ground pole work is something you should add to your riding repertoire. Ground pole work is not only a great activity to spice up your riding in the dreary winter months; it is a great activity no matter the season. From the videos you may have seen of Kelley and Tristan the Wonder Horse on YouTube, you may think that ground pole work might be too difficult for you, but this book will lead you through tips, tricks, and exercises that make ground pole work easy and fun for even beginner riders.

Materials

To ride the exercises in this book you will need:

- **Wooden Poles** – 8 ft. landscaping timbers are the perfect ground poles, and can be purchased from most home improvement stores. Although I prefer 8 ft. poles, 10 ft. and 12 ft. poles can also be used. Landscaping timbers are preferable because they are cut with two flat sides, so they will not roll. Make sure the timbers you choose are straight and free of splinters and cracks. Wooden poles can be sanded if necessary. For the exercises in this book you will need anywhere from four to twenty-eight poles. You can paint your poles in any number of fun colors with outdoor paint to spice up your exercises. Try painting the pole in three even sections, with two different colors, to create a straightness visual for you and your horse.

- **Elevated Poles/Cavaletti** – Solid cavaletties (x cavaletties) can be built or purchased. There are also many products such as plastic blocks, and pole raisers, which can be used to make an average pole into an elevated pole/cavaletti. The elevated pole/cavaletti must always be secured in some way so that the pole does not roll to the ground or out of place when tapped lightly, but will fall if it is hit harder. To learn how to build your own pole raisers, see page twelve.

- **Skinny Poles** – 8 ft. wooden poles can be cut to 5 ft. to make skinny poles.

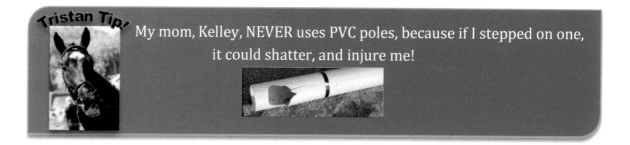

Tristan Tip! My mom, Kelley, NEVER uses PVC poles, because if I stepped on one, it could shatter, and injure me!

Preparation for Ground Pole Exercises

Before attempting the exercises in this book, please ensure your horse is healthy and physically capable of doing ground pole work. If your horse is recovering from an injury, please consult your veterinarian before doing ground pole work. If your horse has never worked over poles before, first try it in hand, by leading your horse over the poles. Always complete a quality warm up including working your horse to achieve a good quality of gait in the walk, trot, and canter.

The Half Halt

Working on establishing good forward transitions prior to pole work will help your horse to be more successful at their first attempts at pole work. Do not be afraid to use half halts to control your horse's tempo (the speed of their rhythm) in your warmup, and through the ground poles. A half halt asks your horse to pay attention. To perform a half halt, sit tall in the saddle with your legs wrapped around your horse for support. Next squeeze the reins for a brief second, slowing the horse's front end down, and then ask your horse to continue on using your seat and leg to create forward motion. When half halting correctly you will be mimicking what you would do to ask for a halt, and then continuing on. During the half halt you should maintain the gait you were riding; if your horse breaks, your half halt was too strong. It should be very brief, only a second or two, before releasing and returning to work. A half halt, will feel like a brief pause, and will allow you to correct or change your horse's tempo and balance. Properly done, it will create suppleness and sensitivity to the leg aids, rebalance your horse, and get your horse's attention. A half halt also asks your horse to sit back on their hind end, resulting in your horse using itself properly.

Starting Over Poles

After you have properly warmed your horse up, you will be ready to move on to some ground pole exercises. Always walk your horse through the exercise before trotting it. When starting ground pole work, practice in an environment that is familiar to your horse, and free of unnecessary distractions, so that your horse can focus on the task at hand.

I love when we ride to music! It helps both of us establish a good rhythm and tempo.

Setting Up Ground Poles

Ground poles need to be set correctly for your horse's stride. This chart will give you an idea of how far apart to set the poles for your horse or pony. Each horse's stride is unique, so you will need to use trial and error to find the right distance for your horse.

Horse/Pony Size	Range for Distance Between Ground Poles (Walking) in Feet and Inches	Range for Distance Between Ground Poles (Walking) in Meters	Range for Distance Between Ground Poles (Trotting) in Feet and Inches	Range for Distance Between Ground Poles (Trotting) in Meters
Small Pony (12.2hh and smaller)	2 feet 6 inches – 2 feet 9 inches	.76 meter – .84 meter	3 feet – 3 feet 3 inches	.91 meter – .99 meter
Medium Pony (12.2hh – 13.2hh)	2 feet 9 inches – 3 feet	.84 meter – .91 meter	3 feet 3 inches – 3 feet 6 inches	.99 meter – 1.06 meter
Large Pony (13.2hh – 14.2hh)	3 feet – 3 feet 3 inches	.91 meter – .99 meter	3 feet 6 inches – 4 feet	1.06 meter – 1.22 meter
Horse	3 feet 3 inches – 3 feet 6 inches	.99 meter – 1.06 meter	4 feet – 4 feet 5 inches	1.22 meter – 1.34 meter

To set your poles, lay a measuring tape down to find your desired distance. Then practice walking that distance off by foot, so that you can estimate by pacing it off, rather than having to use a measuring tape every time.

Basic Ground Pole Configurations

Straight

Start by setting up four poles (you can always start with less and add more if needed). Work on riding through the poles, keeping your horse in the center of the poles. Focus on keeping your horse moving at the same rhythm and tempo through the entire pole set. Once you have mastered four poles, you can add more for a challenge. Riders can choose to sit, post, or two point through any of the exercises in this book. Choose what works best for you and your horse. Remember; always look up and ahead of the poles, because if you look down at them, your horse may think they need to stop to look! Looking up and ahead over poles tells your horse that ground poles are nothing to be worried about. It is a great idea to pick a spot on the horizon or the arena wall to look at, to help remind yourself to keep your eyes up.

Tristan Tip! My favorite color is blue! See how the different colored sections of the poles above all line up? This helps Kelley and I to go straight through our pole sets.

Curved

Curved poles are set on a circle, usually a 20 meter circle. You can easily set your poles on a 20 meter circle with the help of a lunge line. To set them up have a friend, or a sturdy object, stand in the center of your desired circle and hold one end of the lunge line. Hold the other end of the lunge line tight and set your poles with the middle of the pole lining up with the end of the lunge line. This will allow you to set your poles on a 20 meter circle accurately. Walk off your desired pole distance to the center of each pole (from center to center). Make sure each pole is equidistance in the middle, and at both ends. The inside end will have a shorter distance between poles, and the outside end will have a longer distance between poles, compared to the distance in the center. When setting the curved poles always make sure the short side distances are equal, and the long side distances are equal, so the poles ride properly. The tighter the curve of the poles, the tougher the exercise.

Offset

To create offset poles, the center of each pole should be set to your desired distance, while the ends of the poles are pulled in or out to create a zigzag.

Skinny

All of the above exercises can be done with shorter (skinny) poles to challenge straightness and rideability. Like in the photo below, you can always mix skinny and normal poles in an exercise.

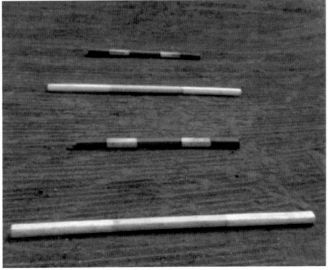

Elevated

Elevating your poles makes any exercise more challenging. The higher you elevate the pole, the more challenging the exercise will be for your horse. Set your poles in your desired pattern, and then elevate the ends (both or every other) to make it more challenging. Standard cavaletti, plastic blocks, or pole raisers can be used to elevate poles. Be sure that whatever you use to elevate your poles secures the pole so it will not easily roll off what it is set on.

 **Tristan Tip!** Kelley makes her own homemade pole raisers by taking a wooden 4x4, cutting a 1 foot section of it, and then cutting a "V" slice into the 1 ft. section where the pole can sit. You can see what they look like in the photo above!

Ground Pole Problems

Rushing/Jumping Poles

Horses often rush through or jump ground poles when they are not confident, lack balance, have inconsistent tempo and rhythm, or are being overwhelmed. To fix these issues, take a step back and reduce the number of poles you are working with. If needed go back to walking and trotting a single pole to regain confidence. If the horse only rushes when faced with multiple poles, work on walking multiple poles. When walking multiple poles, use the walking distances found on page eight. You can also try setting poles nine feet apart so your horse takes trot strides in between each pole. Once your horse is comfortable with this, try putting another pole in the middle, so you have normal pole striding. In the photo below you can see what the nine ft. distance looks like on the left, and then what it will look like with a pole added on the right. When working with a horse who is rushing or jumping poles, be sure to establish a proper half halt (explained on page seven) so that you have a way to ask your horse to pause and pay attention.

Breaking Gait

If your horse breaks to the canter, see the rushing suggestions above. If your horse breaks to the walk, work on keeping your horse moving with energy and impulsion without poles, using an artificial aid such as a crop or spurs if your horse is accustomed to these, or with trainer supervision. Be sure using an artificial aid does not interfere with your rhythm and tempo. Focus on upward transitions to energize your horse. Start back into pole work by keeping your horse trotting over a single pole, and then work back up to multiple poles. Build more energy by picking up the canter and coming back to the trot before the exercise. If your horse seems to want to stop to look at the poles, be sure to look up and ahead, not looking at the poles. If you are looking at the poles, your horse may think it is something they need to look at too!

Tripping

First, ensure your horse is healthy and is not tripping due to a medical issue or hooves that are not well trimmed. Horses often trip because they are on their forehand. When a horse is on their forehand, they are heavy in the front end and lack balance. Ideally, a horse should work from the back end lifting their shoulders. Work on keeping your horse straight through the poles, as well as having an energized trot, good tempo, and rhythm. If focusing on your straightness, energy, rhythm, and tempo does not work, try elevating the poles slightly to make your horse pay attention. Your horse may hit or knock down the pole the first time, but should learn to pick up their feet afterwards to avoid the discomfort of knocking a pole. Remember to use wooden poles, not PVC, as PVC poles can shatter when hit, injuring your horse.

Staying Centered

Use cones or poles to create a lane to help you and your horse visualize the center of the poles.

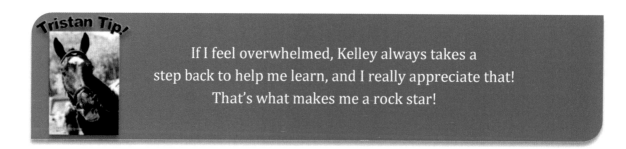

If I feel overwhelmed, Kelley always takes a step back to help me learn, and I really appreciate that! That's what makes me a rock star!

Ground Pole Exercises
Tristan's X Marks the Spot

Materials Needed:

- At least 16, 8 ft. wooden poles.

Objective:

This exercise establishes straightness and helps maintain the rhythm and tempo of the trot. This will also prepare your horse to think quickly and listen to your aids.

Exercise

First, thoroughly warm your horse up on the flat and over a small set of straight ground poles. Then walk your horse though this pole exercise. Next, pick up an energized trot with consistent rhythm and tempo and enter the pole exercise going across the diagonal. This exercise can be ridden as a set of diagonal lines. Use your corners to give your horse a large enough space to make a nice turn into the next diagonal. Avoid making a sharp turn. Focus on maintaining your rhythm and tempo in the gap between the two sets of poles. When the exercise is done, it should look like a figure eight. If you chose to enter the exercise on the blue set of poles, your pattern would be: blue to red, corner, yellow to orange, corner.

Tristan's Y for Yes!

Materials Needed:

- At least 12, 8 ft. wooden poles.

Objective:

This exercise will help your horse to pay attention to your steering. Your horse will need to think quickly and listen to you, as you change direction. Your horse must maintain their rhythm and balance through the turns. When setting up this exercise leave at least eight feet of space between the red set of poles and the yellow and orange sets of poles.

Exercise:

Start by warming up over each pole set (center, left, and right) individually at a trot. To ride this exercise, start by trotting the center set of poles (red) and continuing straight to the rail. Then ask your horse to turn left and trot over the orange set of poles. Proceed to the rail at a trot and track right. Trot all the way to the beginning of your exercise and trot the red poles again. Then continue straight to return to the rail in the end of the ring, tracking right. Finally, turn right to trot the yellow set of poles. You can continue this pattern by tracking left and starting the exercise again.

For another variation, ride the center (red) pole set first, then make a slight left to ride the orange set of poles. Then track right and go deep into the corner. Next ride across the diagonal to trot the yellow set of poles. Finally ride a slight left to ride the red set of poles.

Tristan's Zany Z

Materials Needed:

- At least 12, 8 ft. wooden poles.

Objective:

This exercise will work on progressively increasing the sharpness of turns. This challenges you and your horse to keep good balance and rhythm while navigating tricky turns. If you are having trouble making the tight turns, remember to use your outside aids through the turn to guide your horse around the turn, rather than pulling them around the turn with the inside rein.

Exercise:

Start by warming up over each set of poles individually. Then pick up an energized trot tracking to the right through the end of the ring with the red set of poles. Make a balanced turn to the right and trot the red set of poles. Return to the rail, now tracking left. Trot to the end of the ring, around the green set of poles. Then make a balanced turn out of that corner and trot over the blue set of poles. Return to the rail, now tracking right towards the end of the ring. Then turn off the long side and trot over the green set of poles.

For the ultimate challenge, ride the pole sets like a "Z". Start by tracking right through the corner and riding the red set of poles. Then make a sharp left turn directly to the blue set of poles, and another sharp turn to the right directly to the green set of poles.

Tristan's Squiggle

Materials Needed:

- At least 16, 8 ft. wooden poles.

Objective:

This exercise focuses on changing your horse's bend through the poles. This helps your horse to bend and supple correctly. This also works on interchanging the engagement of the hind legs, as the bend changes, to help with hind end strengthening. When setting up this exercise, leave at least 20 feet of space between the curved pole sets (walking the distance from the middle of each pole, directly from set to set).

Exercise

First, warm your horse up over a small set of curved ground poles. Next, pick up an energized trot with consistent rhythm and tempo, and enter the pole exercise on either end (yellow or blue). As you go through the serpentine (Order: blue, red, orange, and yellow Or: yellow, orange, red, and blue) focus on changing the bend in the gaps between the pole sets, thinking about asking the inside hind leg to step up toward the outside rein. If you are having issues with the change in bend, you can exit the exercises after the first set of poles and reenter it on the last set to introduce the exercise slowly.

To make the Tristan's Squiggle more challenging, you can elevate the outside edge of the curved pole sets. This will make your horse have to work harder to pick up their feet over the poles. It is also a challenge to keep your horse in the center of the poles, as they will want to drift toward the lower end of each pole.

For the ultimate challenge, you can add poles to make the squiggle one continuous set of poles. To create this, add a straight set of four poles between each curved set.

Tristan's Wacky W

Materials Needed:

- At least 8, 8 ft. wooden poles.
- At least 4, 5 ft. skinny wooden poles.

Objective:

This exercise challenges your horse to stay straight through the poles, even with the challenge of offset and skinny poles.

Exercise

First, thoroughly warm your horse up over a small set of offset ground poles, and a small set of skinny poles. Then set up the exercises below and walk your horse though this pole exercise. Next, pick up an energized trot with consistent rhythm and tempo, and enter the pole exercise on either end. The challenge of this exercise is to keep your horse straight, even though he/she is being challenged by the optical illusion of the offset poles. If your horse does not stay straight through the poles, try transitioning back to the walk in the gap between pole sets, and walk the section of the poles they were crooked in.

For a challenge, try elevating the skinny poles by elevating one side of each pole, alternating sides.

For more challenging ideas to transform the Wacky W try:
- Replacing the skinny poles with normal poles (8 ft.) that are elevated.
- Rearranging the poles to two sets of skinny poles and one set of offset poles.
- Replacing the skinny poles with a set of cones to trot straight through.
- Adding more poles for a bigger challenge.

Tristan's Labyrinth

Materials needed:

- At least 12, 8 ft. wooden poles.

Objective:

This exercise challenges you and your horse to maintain straightness. Your horse will take steps in-between the poles in slots 1 and 3, therefore challenging them to maintain their rhythm and tempo. Slot 2 should be set at your horse's normal trot pole striding.

Exercise

To ride this exercise, choose a slot to ride down. Be aware that slots 1 and 3 will ask your horse to take steps between the poles. Make sure that you have a straight approach to your slot. This exercise allows you to be creative and make your own combination! You could go down any slot, and then trot over the poles on the sides to change directions, and then choose another slot.

Tristan's Around the Ring

Materials needed:

- At least 24, 8 ft. wooden poles.

Objective:

This exercise asks horse and rider to ride through a combination of curved and straight poles, as well as changes of direction, while remaining centered in each pole set, and maintaining rhythm and tempo. To create this exercise, set up four curved poles at each end of the arena, four straight poles on each long side, and a set of straight poles on each diagonal.

Exercise

This exercise allows you to build the difficulty as you go along. Start by riding the outside poles sets (straight, curved, straight, curved) in each direction. Once your horse is comfortable with this, try going around the outside once, then using one of the diagonal sets to change direction, and then doing the outside pole sets again in the new direction. We encourage you to be creative! Find ways to use the exercise template to challenge you and your horse. To make this exercise more challenging, try elevating the long side straight pole sets.

Tristan's Crisscross

Materials needed:

- 8, 8 ft. wooden poles.
- 4 pole raisers/stabilizers.

Objective:

This exercise helps your horse to focus on straightness. During the exercise, your horse will need to return to straightness after turning. Practicing this helps teach your horse to be adjustable and listen to your aids. This exercise also works with two elevated poles, which are extra challenging. When setting up this exercise, be sure that you DO NOT just set the middle two blue poles on top of the red poles. Use a pole raiser or improvised device to elevate the poles and secure them (see photo).

Exercise

To begin this exercise, trot over the red set of poles from either direction. Continue straight to the end of the arena, and then choose a direction to turn. Next, turn from the rail to trot over the blue set of poles. Repeat the steps above to complete one repetition of the exercise. Focus on making your turns balanced and smooth, as well as entering the pole sets with straightness.

To make this exercise more difficult, first trot over the red set of poles from either direction. After exiting the red set of poles, turn right away in either direction to face the blue set of poles. Base your turn from the red set of poles to the blue set of poles on the size of a 10 meter circle. Your turn should be round, and not sharp. Then trot straight over the blue set of poles. This smaller turn will be much more difficult. Remember to support your horse with your inside aids, while using your outside aids to ask them to turn. Plan ahead so that you can return to straightness before trotting over the blue set of poles.

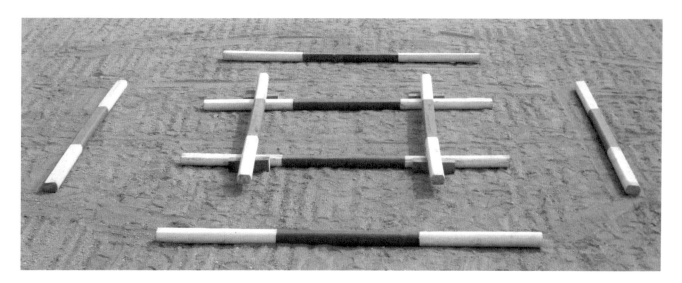

Tristan's Challenge

Have these exercises become too easy for you? Well here are some ideas to make them more challenging!

- Elevate the poles.
- Change out normal poles with skinny poles.
- Try riding the exercise from a different starting point.
- Add more poles to the exercise.
- Combine two exercises.

Tristan Tip! These exercises are just some of the ideas my mom, Kelley, has come up with to challenge me, but you may be able to come up with some ideas yourself! Just remember to keep your horse's safety and fitness level in mind.

Final Thoughts

We hope the exercises in this book have inspired you to try something new with your horse. Horses appreciate variety in their workout just as we do, and we are sure these exercises will help spice up your routine. We encourage you to start slow, and gradually work your way up to trying the more challenging variations of these exercises. If you have worked through these exercises and mastered them, do not worry, we will be releasing an intermediate edition of this book soon with brand new, more challenging exercises!

About the Authors

Tristan Carpe Diem

I am a 2007 Trakehner gelding who loves ground pole exercises! My mom Kelley has known me my  whole life. She worked at the farm where I was born, and assisted with my birth. She knew we would be a perfect pair when she first met me and I walked right up to her to introduce myself. We were like two peas in a pod, and I definitely wanted to be her friend. I was then put up for auction at the farm, as many of the horses were each year. Kelley knew she had to have me, and with a little help from her dad's aggressive bidding, we have been together ever since. Kelley trained me from the beginning to be an obedient and brave horse, and I behave most of the time. We compete in three-day eventing, which is great because I love to jump and show off in the dressage ring! I am not sure exactly what the future holds for us, but we will take it one stride at a time!

Kelley Shetter-Ruiz

As Yoga instructor and graduate of the University of Findlay Equestrian Studies and Equine Business  Management program, Kelley's teaching methods combine the body awareness and alignment developed practicing yoga with the fundamentals of riding. This creates a harmonious union between horse and rider. This philosophy is the basis for Kelley's business Carpe Diem Equestrian Training. With more than 15 years of experience training and teaching, she is knowledgeable in a variety of disciplines including Dressage, Hunter/Jumper, Eventing, and young/green horse work. Kelley's approach to teaching helps her students to become more aware of their own bodies, in order to influence their horse. Her clientele consists of children and adults riding at different levels, and with varying breeds of horses. She has been very involved in 4-H and Pony Club. Her ground pole work videos with her horse, Tristan, have become an internet sensation. Host your own clinic to learn ground pole exercises from Kelley! Kelley is now available to travel for Ground Pole Clinics and Yoga for Equestrians Clinics. For more information about Kelley, and her clinics, see her website: http://carpediemeqtraining.com/.

Breanna Kaho

Breanna is proposal writer by day and amateur dressage rider by night. With Kelley's help, Breanna has

taken her paint horse, Shadow, from extremely unbalanced, to first level dressage horse. Breanna is an active member of the United States Pony Club. She has achieved her HB horse management certification through the USPC. Breanna enjoys sharing her experiences, and giving back, through teaching her fellow Pony Club members. When she is not at the barn, or at her day job, she enjoys creating résumés, flyers, brochures, and even books, for individuals and businesses.

Thank You to Our Supporters

We would like to extend a special thank you to everyone who helped inspire, support, and even edit this book. Our most sincere thanks go out to:

- Cayo Ruiz
- Brenda Roberts
- Mike and Vicki Shetter
- Amelia Kaho
- Matthew Nordseth
- Lauren Zachow
- Erin Teeter

Made in the USA
Middletown, DE
11 August 2020